Scotland's West Coast Fishing

Guthrie Hutton

With stacks of barrels occupying every corner, the herring season at Ullapool must have been in full swing when these fisher lassies were photographed in 1909.

Further Reading

The following were the principal books and websites used by author during his research. *The Real Price of Fish* and *Scotland's East Coast Fishing Industry* are available from Stenlake Publishing; for the rest please contact your local bookshop, reference library or search for them on the internet.

Hallewell, Richard, *Scotland's Sailing Fishermen*, 1991.
Holland, Norman, *Sea Harvest*, 1957.
Hamilton, Forsyth, *Kipper House Tales*, 1986.
Hutchison, Harry, 'The Viking Way', article in *Scottish Field* magazine, March 1957.
Hutchison, Harry, 'Tarbert', article in *Scottish Field* magazine, October 1965.
Fitzpatrick, Linda, *The Real Price of Fish*, 2010.
I'Anson, Mark, *Scotland's East Coast Fishing Industry*, 2009.
Simper, Robert, *Scottish Sail, A Forgotten Era*, 1974.
The Herring Industry Board, *The Story of Herring*, 1969 and 1975.
Thomas, John, *A Regional History of the Railways of Great Britain, Vol. 6 Scotland, The Lowlands and The Borders*, 1971 (revised 1984).
Thomas, John, *The Callander and Oban Railway*, 1966.
Thomas, John, *The West Highland Railway*, 1965.
Vallance, H. A., *The Highland Railway*, 1963.

Acknowledgements

As bombs fell on London during the Second World War my mother returned to Scotland, briefly living in a hut at Sandgreen and catching flounders on lines laid across the beach. That probably counts as the family's closest connection to actual fishing. She moved to Gatehouse of Fleet where I spent my early years and so Kirkcudbright was probably the first fishing harbour I ever saw, although I have to confess to being more familiar with Anstruther in Fife, the home of my uncle, T. Alex Henderson. He played a prominent role in setting up the Scottish Fisheries Museum, which is a wonderful resource and place to visit. In compiling this little book I have tapped memories of those times and the subsequent years when I got to know all of the locations featured in this little book; I hope my recollections are accurate. Richard Stenlake supplied most of the pictures and I am grateful to Alex Young who provided the front cover and inside front cover pictures.

The herring have landed, amidst much activity and excitement on Campbeltown Quay.

Introduction

The Scottish fishing industry is often characterised by images of the big east coast ports, but from the Solway to Stornoway the western coastline, with its numerous inlets and islands, is longer and hosts many harbours with a rich fishing history. A few of these ports, like Ayr can be counted amongst Scotland's oldest burghs. Some, like Campbeltown and Ullapool were developed in later years by landowners and entrepreneurs while others including Mallaig were created through the endeavours of railway companies driving their tracks westward to cash in on the demand for fish in the growing industrial towns and cities. And with large fleets of boats working out of these ports other industries were established like boat building, ice factories, box making and chandleries.

The fishing was carried out in waters as varied as the Irish Sea, the wild Atlantic seaboard and the semi-sheltered Firth of Clyde and yet one species featured almost everywhere, the herring. This ubiquitous little fish was said to actively seek its captors by appearing near to the surface in vast shoals during spawning, but while its presence was well known for centuries, it was not widely fished until after the late 18th century when government bounties allied to industrialised curing practices and better access to markets made it a most valuable fish. The great herring boom was seasonal, leaving time for the pursuit of cod, ling, haddock, halibut and other deep swimming white fish. In shallower water men working from small boats went after crabs, lobsters, langoustine and shellfish including oysters, while others netted salmon and sea trout.

A variety of techniques were deployed. Traditionally these were line fishing and drift netting, but some west coast men developed the controversial ring net that encircled the herring shoals and in more recent times the similar, but vastly bigger purse seine nets have been widely used. Trawling in deeper water and scallop dredging have added to the fishermen's arsenal, but all have contributed to reduced stocks, notably of the once plentiful herring, which has led to legislation limiting catches and some areas of sea bed being declared out of bounds.

Whether they worked in the wide ocean or sheltered loch, the men and boats were never far from danger. The sea can be a harsh environment, the weather in the west can change in an instant and other hazards lurk beneath the waves, all contributing to an industry that was historically regarded as more dangerous than coal mining. The west coast has endured many tragedies. There have been dramatic rescues too, as on the night in 2015 when the Oban lifeboat plucked the five-man crew off the Kirkcudbright-based scallop dredger *St Apollo* moments before she sank in the Sound of Mull*.

Based on a natural resource and the fickle tastes of customers, the fishing industry has had to adapt to meet modern challenges. Boats are fewer, but some are larger and once thriving ports no longer operate at the level they once did. Catches landed by small boats at small harbours travel in large refrigerated lorries to continental Europe and a new business, fish farming has come to proliferate in many sea lochs, all of which has helped to shape the way the fishing industry looks and operates.

*The incident featured in the BBC series on the RNLI, *Saving Lives at Sea*.

The Campbeltown-registered *Maid of Morvern* lying at rest at Waterfoot, Carradale.

The Solway Firth is noted for the rapid rise and fall of its tides and the shallow shelving shores evident in this picture of Waterfoot, on the west bank of the River Annan at the point where it debouches into the broad firth. The river is highly regarded for wild brown trout, but there was also a sea fishery here as the frame, or stance for drying nets indicates. In season, herring skiffs operated as far west as Luce Bay and Annan boats were also engaged in pursuit of shrimps and shellfish. Fish processing on shore enhanced Annan's place in the Solway fishing industry. Improved by an embankment, the port was further developed with jetties and was at one time home to a thriving ship-building industry. It hosted emigrant ships, cargo vessels and steamers plying to and from the Mersey. This latter activity was superseded by the Solway Junction Railway whose mile-long viaduct across the Solway formed a conspicuous feature just upstream from Waterfoot.

The shallow Solway shores meant that some fish could be caught without using a boat at all. Haaf net fishing, seen here being carried out south of Dumfries at Glencaple near the mouth of the River Nith, was a traditional way to catch salmon and sea trout. The net was about sixteen feet in length and supported by poles including one in the middle that divided the net into two pouches. This central pole extended above the top bar forming a lever that the fisherman tipped forward when a fish swam into the net. He then tucked the fish safely into his bag and resumed his stance hoping the next catch would be a salmon: better than sea trout. Men engaged in this activity had to stand in the water as the tide ebbed or flowed past them and drew lots to determine who stood where in the line, so that none would be disadvantaged by always having a poor stance. Haaf netting could also be dangerous. Solway tides came in quickly and it was crucial for men to time their departure correctly because any who stayed too long in a flood tide could struggle to make the shore as their waders filled with water.

Navigating sail-driven craft in shallow tidal rivers like the Dee was never easy, which could account for only one such fishing boat lying alongside Kirkcudbright Harbour in this splendid picture from about 1920. By the 1950s the harbour was virtually disused, but then things changed. It started with one boat, fishing for lobsters and trawling, then others took up the challenge and by the end of the century over a dozen trawlers were working out of the port. Scallop dredging was the main activity with the boats working the beds in the Irish Sea. The activity on the water created work for onshore businesses too in processing, servicing and catering. Then in January 2000 tragedy struck when the Kirkcudbright registered boat *Solway Harvester* got into difficulties in bad weather off the Isle of Man and sank with the loss of the seven-man crew. They all came from the Isle of Whithorn area. It was a shock and a stark reminder that despite the many safety measures introduced over the years, fishing was always and remains a dangerous occupation.

Port William on the east shore of Luce Bay is named after Sir William Maxwell of Monreith who established the village about 1770. Around that time this remote location, with ready access to the Isle of Man and the Antrim Coast, was a hotbed of smuggling. Tobacco, spirits and tea were all shipped across to eager recipients on shore whose activities were often studiously ignored, if not actually supported, by those in authority who just might have found the occasional cask on their doorstep as a reward for turning a 'blind eye'. That changed after 1788 when a barrack house was erected to accommodate soldiers and customs officials and although they too could be 'bought', the smugglers' days were over. People turned to honest endeavours, one of which was fishing and although not a major industry compared to other ports, some boats evidently used the harbour as this picture from about 1950 shows. Creel fishermen using smaller boats continue to work out of the harbour.

Situated on the west coast of the Rhinns of Galloway, Portpatrick is the closest point to Ireland on the British mainland and in the early 19th century a lot of money was spent to make the harbour fit for boats to operate across the North Channel. Despite all that it remained a difficult harbour exposed to prevailing winds and swell, but Victorian entrepreneurs were determined people and by 1862 a railway had been pushed in stages across Galloway from Dumfries, reaching Portpatrick in 1862. It didn't immediately change the port's fortunes, with a packet boat service starting in 1868 and lasting for only a few years, but it did make a difference to the fishing trade. Having, for some years, eschewed herring in favour of line-caught cod, local fisherman suddenly found they had a new market in the big cities where Portpatrick cod became recognised as a premium fish. Here one of the small boats engaged in this activity is seen landing its catch with the men carrying some very big fish up the harbour-side steps.

Some big cod are again prominent in this picture, with the men, perhaps a little reluctantly, posing for the photographer with their catch. Behind them and the rather untidy pile of boxes, is the lifeboat station. A lifeboat was first based at Portpatrick in 1877 and many fishermen over the years, perhaps including those in the picture, will have formed part of the crews. Beyond the harbour they faced a hostile sea attending many 'shouts', including to fishing boats, receiving one silver and two bronze medals, and many citations for their bravery. Perhaps the most newsworthy call-out occurred on 31st January 1953 when the ferry *Princess Victoria*, sailing from Stranraer to Larne with 125 passengers and 49 crew on board, foundered in a fearsome storm. Braving very rough seas the lifeboat saved two people, but 133 died in one of Britain's worst maritime disasters. It was a historically bad weather event with boats sunk, a fishing community in north east Scotland wrecked and a North Sea storm surge that flooded parts of eastern England and inundated large areas of Holland.

The railway that reached Portpatrick in 1862 also served Stranraer, which was likewise able to capitalise on the advantages of sending fish to distant city markets. Cod again seems to have been a favoured species if this picture of men gutting the fish on the harbour side is any indication. Railway access and the port's situation on the sheltered waters of Loch Ryan also gave Stranraer clear advantage over Portpatrick in the days of steam and it soon became the favoured location for the Irish ferries. The loch was also a more varied fishing ground for local boats with skate, flounders, cod, haddock, whiting and the occasional turbot being caught along with migratory salmon and sea trout. Herring in season were also landed at Stranraer. Crabs and lobsters filled many a creel, but the shellfish that the loch became famous for were oysters. These gastronomic delicacies are held in such high regard that in September 2017 the first Stranraer Oyster Festival was held to mark the start of the season for harvesting the wild native oyster beds.

Stranraer Harbour is seen here with a boat alongside bearing the registration letters BF for Banff on the north east coast, so she was a long way from home. The registration of fishing boats, with distinctive letters and numbers was introduced following the British White Herring Act of 1860. All boats fishing out of ports in the UK, which included Ireland at the time, had to display their registration number on each bow painted in white on a black ground, and in a contrasting colour on the sail and later, for steam-powered boats, on funnels. Most ports were identified with the first and last letters of the port name, as in SR for Stranraer, or the first two letters, OB for Oban, while some used three letters, like BRD for Broadford on Skye. Some ports were identified by single letters and of these the ones most likely to appear on Scotland's west coast were Irish like D for Dublin or B for Belfast, although Aberdeen's A was a familiar sight in some harbours. There were two ports of registry on the Solway coast, Dumfries (DS) and Wigtown (WN).

One of the west coast's more ubiquitous boat registrations was, indeed still is, BA for the little South Ayrshire village of Ballantrae. The harbour there was developed in the mid 19th century with a substantial L-shaped breakwater, topped by a solid sea wall to protect sheltering vessels. The Board of Fisheries met half the cost of the development, giving the village a status reflected in its position as a port of registry, but sadly for Ballantrae, not in the development of a fishing fleet. One big reason for this was because the village was never connected to a railway whereas Girvan, just a few miles up the coast was, when the Glasgow and South Western Railway (G&SWR) reached the town in 1860. With Stranraer Harbour also connected in 1862 a trade war broke out with horse-drawn carts of the G&SWR taking fish landed at Ballantrae north to Girvan and the Caledonian Railway carting fish south to Stranraer. It was an arrangement that consigned Ballantrae to a secondary role and as it dwindled the other ports prospered, especially Girvan, which is seen here with an array of fish laid out for sale on the quayside.

Backed by the rolling Ayrshire hills and with special views across the Firth of Clyde to Ailsa Craig, Girvan occupies a superb setting, yet struggled to match it in the late 18th century when a traveller described its houses as 'huts more miserable than those of Ballantrae'. The harbour at the mouth of the Girvan Water was also, like many river harbours, hampered by a shallow entrance. Improvements in the mid 19th century eased the problems and readied the port to take advantage of the commercial possibilities brought by the railway. The fishing industry, which hitherto had not fully exploited the immediate waters, grew rapidly with boats venturing further out to take advantage of cod, mackerel, and an abundance of herring in season, as this picture from about 1910 shows. Shore-based industries also thrived including the boatyard of Alexander Noble & Sons, which developed from traditional wooden boats to ones made of steel. Despite all that, railway access ensured that the fish trade didn't have the harbour to itself, with the products of agriculture, and coal from the pits in the Girvan Valley, also being handled.

The coast south of Ayr is rugged and beautiful, but prone to being periodically battered by heavy seas driven on by westerly winds and presenting a challenge to seafarers that is compounded by a lack of natural harbours, although there is one little haven, Dunure. It consists of a square basin lined with masonry quays entered by way of a channel cut through rock in the early 19th century. Buildings set beside the basin add to the image of a delightful fishing village overlooked by the ruins of a castle with 13th century origins, a former stronghold of the Kennedys, Earls of Cassillis. As this photo from about 1910 shows, local fishermen made good use of the harbour following its development and their options for getting catches to market improved in 1906 when a railway was opened between Alloway Junction and Girvan, even 'though the line was situated on high ground above the village. About 30 boats were still working up to the 1960s, but by that time vessels were getting bigger and, as they moved to larger ports, Dunure, like other small harbours, became the preserve of small boats and leisure craft.

Herring lie on the deck of this boat while a loaded creel is swung up to the quayside. A small crowd has gathered to watch, or perhaps to buy. Enriched by the warming effect of the Gulf Stream the Firth of Clyde had it all: a rocky shore for shellfish; cod, haddock and other demersal fish that feed near the sea bed; and plankton-eating pelagic fish close to the surface and of these the most prized was herring. At between eight and fifteen inches long, it isn't big, but because it swims in shoals can be caught in huge numbers. It is highly nutritious and for centuries presented such a valuable source of food that governments tried to encourage fisher folk to go out and catch as many as they could. These measures didn't always work because they were initially aimed at rewarding large boats, but in the late 18th century, when the emphasis shifted to paying a bounty for the size of catch, the herring industry took off and continued to expand for over a hundred years. Ports around the Clyde took full advantage although this evocative image of Dunure from about 1910 shows the small scale of activity there compared to larger places like Ayr.

With salmon in the Rivers Ayr and Doon, and abundant fish in the firth, Ayr served the markets of Greenock, Glasgow and surrounding towns and was at one time the pre-eminent fishing port on the Clyde Coast. This dominance goes back hundreds of years, possibly even to 1205 when Ayr became a Royal Burgh, and although its position began to slide with the development of steam navigation it was still important enough to be made a port of registry identified by the letters AR. Originally the harbour was little more than a tidal basin, but was improved with the removal of the tidal bar at the river mouth, and then the development of quays along both banks and a dock on each side of the river. The North Dock was mainly used by industry, including for the export of coal, a commodity closely identified with Ayrshire. The fish market was located on the South Quay where these boats were photographed in 1959. Boats were still landing fish when the mining industry ceased and at that time Ayr might have looked forward to a future based on former fishing glories, but the dream was thwarted in 1996 when Associated British Ports decided that, instead of redeveloping the old fish market, they would build a new one up the coast at Troon

North of the county town, there were three other Ayrshire ports of registry for fishing boats, Troon TN, Irvine IE and Ardrossan AD, although fish may not be the first trade people would popularly associate with them. Troon was developed to handle coal transported to it on the pioneering Kilmarnock and Troon Railway. Irvine was more diverse, but again coal was a big part of the mix. Ardrossan was planned as a transhipment port for the Glasgow, Paisley and Ardrossan Canal, but that got only as far west as Johnstone and again coal shipments became central to the port's activities. Saltcoats Harbour, seen here about 1900, was also initially intended to handle coal. It was developed between 1685 and 1700 by local landowner Robert Cunninghame who wanted a facility close to his Auchenharvie Colliery from where he could ship its coal to Ireland. It evidently also proved handy for these skiffs engaged in the Clyde herring fishery, all of which, at least all that are visible, show the registration letters for Ardrossan, which wasn't just a port of registry, but bigger, better equipped and situated just over a mile to the north it eventually eclipsed the old Saltcoats Harbour for both the coal and fishing industries.

Of all the herring caught in the Clyde, those taken from Loch Fyne, a sea loch that opened off the north west corner of the firth, came to be prized above all others. Boats from around the firth engaged in the fishery, but the best-placed port was Tarbert on the east side of the Kintyre peninsula. The town is clustered around the head of East Loch Tarbert, which opens off Loch Fyne and although not large is semi-enclosed by headlands and two small islands making it a wonderful natural harbour. Before acquiring fame as a fishing port, Tarbert evidently had an earlier role indicated by an ancient castle that sits on the southern shore above the pier. Its history was also shaped by its location on the narrow neck of land that separated East Loch Tarbert from West Loch Tarbert and was used as a land bridge by the Vikings, and seen as a possible canal link across the peninsula to the west coast. It was claimed that such a canal would benefit the fishing industry, but it was never made and fishing prospered anyway helping Tarbert to grow into the town seen here in this 1951 view looking across the harbour to the Parish Church with its prominent tower and crown steeple.

Loch Fyne men are generally credited with developing the fishing method known as ring netting, which they adapted from a technique originally used for salmon fishing. With one end of the net attached to the shore they rowed the other end out in a wide loop before bringing it back in, trapping the encircled fish. At sea, they worked their boats in pairs. One would shoot the net and work round in a semi-circle while the other boat picked up the end of the net and brought it back to the first boat, completing a circle, as they would formerly have done from land. Having closed the ring, both crews hauled the catch aboard one boat. Working in relatively sheltered waters the boats were small clinker-built skiffs with a keel of about 25 feet and a beam of about nine feet. The stem (the foremost edge of the bow) was nearly vertical and the stern, which sat more deeply in the water, was steeply raked making the boat highly manoeuvrable. Some of these skiffs are seen here identified with Tarbert's distinctive TT registration letters. Net drying stances line the shore.

Skiffs had a raked mast and when these little boats left Tarbert Harbour with jib and lug sail set it was apparently a glorious sight. Conventional drift net fishermen were unimpressed. They believed that ring netting took too many fish compared to the way they worked. Drifters did what the name implies, their crews shot a long, deep curtain of net, which hung in the water suspended from floats and as the boat drifted with the tide the fish that swam into the net were caught by the gills. Angered by ring netters' large catches, they lobbied friends in parliament to have the practice stopped. A ban was imposed in 1851, but ten years later it was lifted and the nimble little skiffs got back to work. The ban was a serious deterrent, but while they had to heed government dictum, Tarbert men were apparently unconcerned about upsetting a higher authority and went fishing on a Sunday, although just for luck liked to have their boat's tiller made of rowan wood! But over time stocks were depleted and even one of the humorous *Para Handy* stories published in the early 20th century noted the disappearance of herring from Loch Fyne.

A veritable forest of masts is presented by this fleet of skiffs in Campbeltown Harbour, at the foot of the Kintyre peninsula. Some of these boats are decked or half-decked, a later development that gave crews some shelter from the elements, which was always a consideration for the men on these little boats. As well as having some protection on board the hull shape meant that skiffs were swift and could run for port or even be rowed if necessary if the weather turned nasty while they were at sea. And that must have been doubly important working at the southern end of Kintyre where the sea could be rough and shelter from the land minimal. The boats are sitting alongside the town's Old Quay. Work on it began in 1722, but was not completed until 1765 by which time construction of the New Quay was under way to form a semi-enclosed harbour basin. Further improvements and extensions were carried out in the late 19th century.

Campbeltown is not a very old settlement, nor is it particularly Highland, despite its location. Its establishment arose out of King James VI's desire to pacify disputatious Highlanders. In 1607 he granted the former Clan Donald lands in Kintyre to their bitter enemy the 7th Earl of Argyle on condition that he establish a settlement and populate it with industrious lowlanders. Argyle did just that, giving the new burgh his own family name. The newly planted community repaid the favour by setting up weaving, mining and salt-making industries. Distilling came later and had the wish in the popular song for Campeltown Loch to be composed of whisky and drunk dry, it would have deprived the fishing industry of a superb natural harbour. Sheltered by Davaar Island, the harbour was further enhanced by the building of the Old and New Quays. The former is seen here with the Royal Hotel of 1907 in the background at the pier head and the foreground filled with a very large stack of herring barrels.

Once thought to migrate round the coasts of Britain, the herring shoals were later shown to differ one from another and these appeared in various places at different times of the year. One of those places was the Firth of Clyde, with Campbeltown well placed to take advantage. The industry made good use of the Old Quay, as is evident from this picture showing gutting troughs, known as farlans, in the foreground filled with fish brought in by the steam drifters in the background. The photographer has done well to persuade the women gutters to delay their work and pose for the picture because they had to clear the farlan quickly and time was precious. The herring they gutted were not destined for the fresh fish markets, but for the curing industry that grew massively through the late 19th and early 20th centuries to become a seasonal feature of many ports around the British Isles. The women did a tough, back-breaking job working in teams of three of which two, each wielding a sharp knife at great speed gutted the fish while the third packed them into the barrels along with copious quantities of salt. They often wrapped rags around their fingers to protect them from the flashing blade or the salt, or both.

Many boats bearing the Campbeltown registration of CN were based at the little village of Carradale situated between Campbeltown and Tarbert on the east side of the Kintyre peninsula and seen here in a picture from 1938. At this point Kintyre looks east across the Kilbrannan Sound to the island of Arran, a view that people from the village have enjoyed for centuries. Initially this was a community based on crofting and fishing, but over the years fishing assumed greater importance despite a lack of harbour facilities requiring boats to draw up on the shore at Waterfoot. The first pier, built in 1858, was improved a dozen years later when an iron pier was erected with a higher level for steamers and a lower one for fishing boats. A new pier-cum-harbour wall, seen on the facing page, was built in 1960 giving boats greater protection, but as the species that formerly maintained the fishing fleet have diminished so have the number and size of boats which have shifted focus to shellfish and prawns. The harbour also acts as a base for the boats working at a large salmon farm about a mile to the north – is that the new fishing industry?

A particularly poignant tragedy affected Carradale in November 1990 when the nets of the locally based trawler, *Antares* were snagged by the submarine, HMS *Trenchant*. *Antares* was fishing in the deep Arran Trench, off the north east coast of the island and had set her nets at 60 metres. The submarine's crew, on an intensive training exercise, thought their boat was operating at sufficient depth to avoid any problems, but they were wrong, the trawler capsized and went down with the loss of all four men on board. Hours elapsed before the navy realised what had happened and at the subsequent enquiry all blame was apportioned to them. Typically submarines are big, weighing over 5,000 tons, and when submerged can represent a significant danger so after this incident new regulations were brought in to keep them away from fishing boats while submerged, although incidents still occur. The Royal Navy has been based in the Clyde since before the First World War when they used Lamlash Bay off Arran as a fleet anchorage with easy access to the north Atlantic. That combination of sheltered haven close to strategically important waters has ensured the navy's continued presence, although their ships, both during and after the Second World War, have mainly been submarines.

Boats powered with petrol or diesel engines started to take over from the sailing skiffs just before the First World War and became more common after the war. This increased the ring netters' capacity to travel further and catch more as might be indicated by this group of boats thought to have been photographed at Brodick, Arran in 1936. They all bear either Tarbert or Campbeltown registrations and of the latter one is known to have been a Carradale boat, which could indicate that some of the others were also from there. The likelihood too is that they were all working together. They look quite old, even for the time, and one Tarbert boat has no wheelhouse but provision for tiller steering, and they are all festooned with old tyres as fenders. What they also show is that the practice of ring netting continued through the mid 20th century until the fears of the 19th century drift netters came true. By 1980 the herring had largely disappeared from the Clyde.

Arran has long attracted fishermen – too long for some. It all looks quiet in this picture of Lamlash, with an elderly puffer and one small skiff at the pier, but by the end of the 20th century concerns were growing that scallop dredging and overfishing were damaging the seabed and the island's marine environment. This prompted the formation of the Community of Arran Seabed Trust, a charity, which with the aid of scientific research campaigned to establish a 'no take zone' in Lamlash Bay. Their efforts came to fruition in 2008, since when the initial zone has been extended to cover the larger South Arran Marine Protected Area. Subsequent monitoring has revealed a significant recovery and increased diversity of fish and shellfish. Scallops are more numerous and larger, as are other shellfish and lobsters, and shoals of juvenile cod and whiting are also recovering. This initiative is not just of significance for Arran and the Clyde, but has implications for worldwide fisheries where the demand for seafood has depleted stocks.

Less precipitate and more verdant than Arran, the Clyde's other large island, Bute, has a long history of fishing as the registration letters RO for Rothesay displayed on these skiffs shows. Named *Brothers* and *Psyche*, they are drawn up on the shore at Port Bannatyne, a couple of miles to the north of Rothesay. Boats like these fished for herring at night when the shoals appeared almost fluorescent allowing even little boats to make big catches. With fish on board they would not be able to get quickly to port, so boats working across the Clyde developed a system whereby they shone a light to attract the fish carriers, simple screw-propelled steam vessels like puffers. The crews of both boats would then agree a price and transfer the herring to the steamer, which raced to the nearest railhead, often Greenock, and a train to Glasgow. By this arrangement the fish reached the market quickly so that people in the city could have the freshest possible herring – 'Glasgow Magistrates', the biggest, plumpest fish, fetched the highest prices. Loch Long, Loch Goil and other Clyde lochs also provided rich pickings for boats from Greenock or Port Glasgow, which had their own registrations GK and PGW.

Rothesay, the principal town on Bute, is clustered around a north-facing bay sheltered from prevailing winds. It had a booming herring fishery by the mid 18th century coinciding with the construction of the Old Quay. The New Quay was added toward the end of the century and subsequent additions and improvements have provided the town with an extensive harbour. By the mid 19th century over 550 boats were working, crewed by an average of three men or boys each, which suggests they were mainly skiffs. They were made on the island in a couple of boatyards. Some fish were sold fresh, but mostly they were cured and despatched in thousands of locally made barrels. It was a huge industry providing a lot of employment, but as the century progressed Bute, with its favourable climate and almost idyllic location found another source of income catering for shoals of tourists from Glasgow and other industrial towns. Fishing continued although not all the boats using the harbour were local, as is clear from this picture showing Leith registered boats. They probably got to Bute through the Forth & Clyde Canal.

Stretching from Grangemouth in the east to Bowling on the Clyde, the Forth & Clyde Canal was completed in 1790. It closed on the stroke of midnight as 1962 gave way to 1963, with the last sea-to-sea passage being that of a fishing boat returning to the east coast. Latterly fishing boats were the principal users of the canal. Sometimes boats from the west went east, with a few venturing a long way south down England's east coast, but more usually it was east coast boats, especially from the Lothians and Fife that ventured west in pursuit of late season Clyde herring. Salt water fishermen using the canal in winter sometimes had to contend with one of the hazards of fresh water; ice. Here the *Providence* of St Monans in Fife has been caught in freezing conditions at Maryhill in Glasgow and the crew are trying to protect their wooden hull at the waterline by hanging sheets of iron around it. If conditions allowed, the canal's ice-breaker *Clydeforth* would clear a path for boats following in her wake.

Glasgow may not be thought of as a centre for fishing, although it was a port of registry and the location of a major fish market. A market had existed, probably for centuries, before it was located in new premises in the Bridgegait in 1872-73. It was later extended, taking in the distinctive 17th century steeple of the former Merchants' House, one of the city's historical architectural gems. The market moved to a new location at Blochairn in 1977 and the old market was revamped as a retail outlet, and when that failed it became a music venue.

Facing page: Boat crews using the canal courted popularity with bridge and lock keepers by giving them some fish as they passed through. Others stopped to sell fish to local people as the Leith registered *Harvester* has done here at Clydebank – cod appears to be on offer. Judging from the small crowd that has gathered, people must have known about the boat's arrival, so this may have been a regular occurrence – and modern supermarkets would struggle to compete with the freshness of fish bought this way. As is evident from the *Harvester*, and the *Providence*, boat crews often used old tyres as boat fenders; they cost nothing but were not popular with the canal authorities because if they fell off in a lock they could block the gates. Another reason why boats were brought into the canal was to have their engines serviced and repaired at the Bergius Company works at Port Dundas. Founded in 1904, the company was an early pioneer in building cars, but soon turned to boats latterly making the highly successful Kelvin Marine diesel engines that were fitted in many fishing boats.

While the Forth & Clyde Canal offered a route through to the west for east coast boats, the Crinan Canal provided a way to go further west without having to face the hazardous passage around the Mull of Kintyre. This was certainly one of the main considerations for making the canal along with the stimulus it would provide for the fishing industry. Only nine miles long, it ran across the top of Knapdale, from Loch Gilp, which opens off Loch Fyne, to Crinan in the west. Ardrishaig, the village that grew up at the eastern end of the canal, also became a significant centre for the Loch Fyne herring fishery. Net drying stances, set out beside the canal, were one of the features of the village. So too was Munro's boat yard, where many of the skiffs that worked out of Ardrishaig were built. Seen here in a picture from 1891, it was situated on the canal between locks 3 and 4, so all of its reputedly good sea boats started out on fresh water. Ardrishaig was also noted for its smokehouse where some of the herring were transformed into the equally famous Loch Fyne kippers. And when the herring season was over, Ardrishaig fishermen turned to short line fishing.

Work to construct the canal began in 1794. It opened in 1801, but that moment of optimism didn't last, being followed by a succession of closures, breaches, re-openings and improvements that continued on and off until the canal was finally complete in 1817. Whether or not it had a transformative effect on the fishing industry it was certainly well used by fishing boats as is evident in this picture of Crinan harbour in the 1960s. Ardrishaig fishermen tended to stick to the loch, but larger boats from Tarbert and around the Clyde Coast, like these Ballantrae registered boats from Girvan, are typical of those that went further west through the canal. The basin at the western end of the canal had been made deliberately large to encourage development of a local industry, but served mainly as a stop-off point for transiting boats from distant ports, often jostling for space with those ubiquitous west coast workhorses, the puffers. The Crinan Hotel sits beside the basin and boat crews might have enjoyed the distraction of the bar, while more up-market guests savoured locally sourced seafood.

Currents and eddies in the tidally turbulent Sound of Jura tugged at the helm of boats heading west out of Crinan to the Firth of Lorn, with Oban to the north. Blessed by a superb natural harbour sheltered by the island of Kerrera, Oban developed into a place of great significance to trade and communications, and yet, as a town, it isn't very old. Dunollie Castle at the entrance to Oban Bay testifies to historic occupation, but other than a scatter of crofting settlements little existed until the mid 18th century when local proprietors led by the Duke of Argyll set about encouraging development. A customs house, other buildings and developments in trade started the process. The opening of the Crinan and Caledonian Canals by the 1820s placed the town on trade routes between the Clyde and Inverness that had hitherto not existed, and shipping to and from the Hebridean islands expanded massively. Two piers, one on the south side of the bay, the other to the north, boosted trade and local industry. Burgh status was granted in 1820, parliamentary burgh status followed; in little more than a few decades Oban, seen here in the 1930s, had come from virtually nothing to being arguably the west coast's most important port.

Fishing was initially seen as important and contributed to exports, but the town was a long way from the lucrative markets of Glasgow and surrounding area, which inhibited the trade in a perishable commodity like fish. Unable to develop, it languished, but despite the difficulties Oban was recognised as a port of registry with the identifying letters OB. Then, at the end of June 1880, the geographical disadvantage disappeared with the opening of the Callander and Oban Railway. It was a somewhat indirect route to Glasgow, going by way of Stirling, so it wasn't fast, but it was a lot quicker than anything that had gone before. Almost immediately the railway company was bidding for business from as far away as Stornoway to be brought by fast steamer to Oban for onward transit, which caused consternation for the contractor trying to finish building the new railway pier. This trade challenged the Highland Railway's existing line west from Inverness, which had previously enjoyed a monopoly, so they retaliated by cutting rates, but the Oban line had made its point; it was in the business of carrying fish. East coast boats were soon fishing the waters around Skye and delivering bumper catches to Oban. Glasgow fish merchants were delighted.

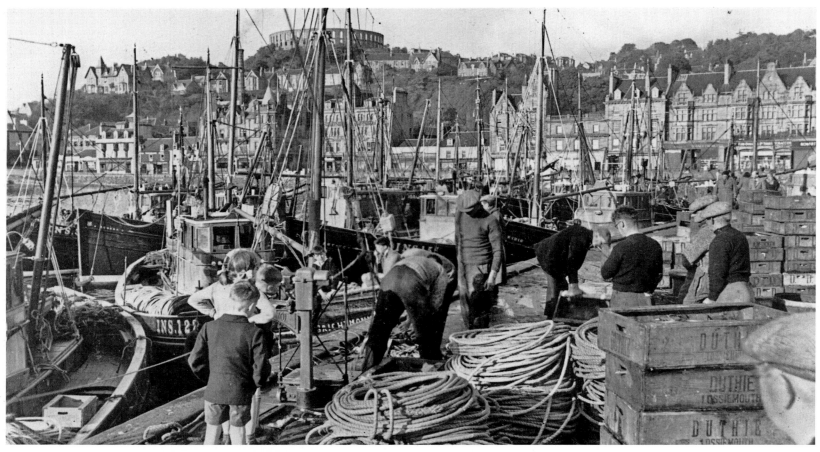

The east coast boats' arrival was no coincidence. They had been encouraged to come to the west by the Callander and Oban Railway's manager, John Anderson. Local boats traditionally fished for herring in the summer, but Anderson wanted to develop winter traffic on the railway and the east coast men were happy to oblige, but they deployed trawl nets, only recently legalised, which caused great concern to west coast fishermen who feared that the heavy catches being landed at Oban would destroy fish stocks. An excitable Glasgow journalist disagreed and urged the Oban men to exploit the waters around Mull, making the somewhat hyperbolic suggestion that the seas there were so full of fish that it would be difficult to row a boat through them! Anderson also tried to encourage exploitation of the heavy shoals of mackerel, a fish often regarded at the time as a nuisance, all part of an endeavour to maximise the fish traffic, which because of its unpredictability could not be easily timetabled. The railway even developed a system to let fish trains run when the line was shut during the night. East coast boats and boxes are evident in this picture, with the distinctive landmark of McCaig's Tower in the background.

East coast boats seeking west coast riches were frequent users of the Caledonian Canal. Designed by the great engineer Thomas Telford, construction began in 1803 and the canal was opened in 1822, but then closed again between 1844 and 1847 to be improved and deepened. It ran from Inverness to the western sea lock at Corpach on Loch Eil, just west of where it and Loch Linnhe converge as a single body of water. A large basin was cut from solid rock at Corpach to provide a harbour where crews could rest before venturing further, although fishermen didn't usually hang around and often flouted canal speed limits to get through quickly, because time spent in the canal was time not fishing and thus not earning. One section of canal where boats were routinely delayed was the flight of eight locks at Banavie where these boats were being admired in the 1930s by some Boy Scouts; Loch Eil can be seen in the distance. Fort William, just around the head of the loch from Banavie and Corpach, was not a noted fishing port, but it did have a railway, which became much more important for the transport of fish when the line was extended across the Caledonian Canal to Mallaig.

The West Highland Railway got to Fort William in 1894 but, with the giant North British Railway Company behind it, always had the ambition of pushing on to the more lucrative fishing grounds on the Atlantic Coast. The company's first choice for a western terminal was Roshven on Loch Ailort, but when the local landowner rejected the idea, they were forced to look elsewhere, eventually settling on Mallaig, a scarcely populated site on the tip of North Morar. Construction work began in 1897 under the direction of contractor 'Concrete Bob' McAlpine who built some spectacular viaducts, and other smaller structures, with mass concrete. The use of this new medium allowed him to move quickly and economically, completing the line in April 1901. A new pier was also pushed out from the shore to enhance the natural harbour and start the process of creating a new fishing port. Initially there was no local fleet and Mallaig was too new to be a port of registry, but it grew rapidly with boats from elsewhere – the ones in this picture are all from east coast ports – coming in to land their catches, which were speedily despatched south with fish vans attached to the rear of passenger trains.

Registered at Aberdeen and Fraserburgh, the boats on the facing page are all steam drifters, a type of vessel often seen in west coast ports, but rarely west coast owned. Marine steam engines had been in existence for many years before their first use in a fishing vessel in the 1880s. Sail-driven craft could outrun steam in favourable conditions, but struggle in adverse weather while a steamer could always make harbour, yet it took a while for the industry to adapt and work out how best to use steam. The principal drawback was cost, because steam-powered boats needed coal and two additional members of crew to work the engine and attend to the boiler, and they were paid a wage rather than taking a share of the catch, good or bad. Through the first decade of the 20th century the number of steam drifters grew steadily adding huge catching capacity during the herring boom of that time. Through the 1930s steam began to lose its appeal as motor power in the form of petrol or diesel engines began to be installed in boats like the one in this picture, older sailing craft were also adapted, but steamers had to be scrapped. Either way the railway profited, because it delivered coal to Mallaig for steam engines and oil for the diesels – and carried away the fish.

Gaining access to the lucrative fish trade prompted railway companies to make determined efforts to push their tracks through to the west coast. The first to succeed was the Dingwall & Skye Railway, which opened to Strome Ferry in 1870. The company had intended to go on to Kyle of Lochalsh, but financial difficulties forced them stop ten miles short. Importantly they had reached the west coast and cargoes of fish began to move east by rail. They didn't move anywhere one Sunday in 1883 when local people, determined that the Sabbath should be observed, took over the pier and station and prevented boats from landing their catches. Police and railway officials were powerless to stop the protest, which duly ended at midnight. That wasn't the only problem; some skippers didn't like landing their catch at Strome because currents and rocks in Loch Carron made the approach to the pier difficult. Having taken over from the Dingwall & Skye in 1877, the Highland Railway Company, resolved to finish the line to Kyle and, despite significant engineering challenges, they did just that by November 1897. Kyle became a busy fishing port, complete with ancillary industries like this large smokehouse and kipper factory.

Kyle of Lochalsh is perhaps better known as the point from where ferries, and since 1995 the bridge, crossed over to the Isle of Skye. The island was noted for the abundance of fish in its surrounding waters, but it had no great fishing port. Broadford, identified by the letters BRD, was a port of registry and boats worked out of Portree and Isleornsay on the Sleat peninsula, but the scope for supplying more than local needs was limited, essentially because Skye was an island close to the mainland. Despite that, one place was singled out for development as a fishing station, Stein on Vaternish, formerly known as Lochbay. It was one of four locations chosen by the British Fisheries Society, a joint stock company formed in 1786 from a committee of the Highland Society of London. They aimed to encourage a fishing industry in the north and west of the country and engaged the great Thomas Telford to design a harbour and street layout for the proposed Lochbay village, but the scheme had been misjudged. Crofters showed little enthusiasm for fishing, and almost coincidentally the herring shoals deserted the waters off the north of Skye. The scheme was abandoned, but the terrace of houses shown in this picture was built some years later on the line proposed by Telford.

The British Fisheries Society was formed following a lecture delivered by a speaker whose travels in the north of Scotland had convinced him that if a string of villages could be set up around the west and north coasts, that would encourage local people to develop a fishing industry. Fired with enthusiasm, the Society set about raising money and assessing places where these ideas could be put into practice, eventually reducing their grand vision to just four locations, Lochbay, Tobermory on Mull, Pulteneytown (Wick), on the north east coast, and Ullapool on Loch Broom. The results were mixed; Lochbay never got going and Tobermory didn't work as a fishing port despite having an excellent harbour that made it an ideal island capital. Of the other schemes Wick prospered hugely during the herring boom years, and although it struggled to begin with Ullapool developed into a place of some significance and a port of registry identified as UL. The new settlement showed early promise but progress was initially hampered by remoteness from markets and then devastated by the sudden disappearance of herring shoals from local waters. That could have spelled the end, but when the British Fisheries Society sold out in the 1840s the fortunes of the village began to revive. Barrels, boats and bustle suggest that the herring fishery had returned by 1909 when this picture was taken.

Herring continued to be important up to and beyond the Second World War when east coast boats equipped with echo sounders, and scooping up vast quantities of fish in purse seine nets, landed fish by the lorry load to be driven away for processing. The seine net's rapacious capacity effectively ended the herring fishery by the 1970s. That coincided with the arrival in Loch Broom of Scandinavian Klondikers, large factory ships which true to the gold-rush origins of the name sought to buy up and process large stocks of fish. Ships from other nations, especially Russia, also arrived to sit on the loch for months on end buying up fish, especially mackerel. It was a bonanza for them, and also for local shopkeepers who suddenly found they had a large number of free-spending new customers camped on their doorstep. Eventually all that activity sailed away, leaving Ullapool with a relatively small local fleet pursuing prawns, lobsters, crabs and scallops, and for the first time in a century, a sustainable fishery. It also became the terminal for the Stornoway ferry, and thus a key location in the country's transport infrastructure.

Long before the 19th century herring boom, boats working out of Stornoway pursued cod, ling, haddock and other white fish species with baited lines, a traditional form of fishing practised all round the Scottish coast. The lines could be a mile or more long with hooks tied on at regular intervals. Baiting hooks was a laborious, time-consuming job, often done by women. Far removed from markets, the islanders were always at a disadvantage and so while some fish will have been consumed locally, much of the catch was dried and salted for sale on the mainland. No one gave the abundant herring shoals, which appeared off the islands in May and June, much thought or minded when large Dutch busses scooped them up and sailed away to foreign shores. But when the herring boom began, the impact on Stornoway was huge. The season began when the curers arrived to set up the shore-based operation, quickly followed by boats from the north and east of Scotland and England. As landings increased, the need to replace quayside bartering with an organised fish market was met when the octagonal building seen here was opened in 1897. Demolished in the 1970s, it was replaced on site by a new steamer terminal that echoed the distinctive shape.

With Stornoway at the centre of the herring boom, island fishermen might have seemed well placed to share in the riches, but again they were often at a disadvantage compared to their east coast counterparts. Always the poor relations, they usually didn't have the cash to buy their boats, so had to borrow from the curers and rarely made enough money to do anything other than repay their debts. Consequently they always tended to be working with older boats, so by the time the islanders could boast of having the finest sail fishing craft ever built, the east coast boats were steam-driven, as can be seen in this picture looking across the decks of Stornoway registered boats to east coast drifters in the background. These foreground boats were indeed very fine sailing craft built to a design known as the Fifie, a name that clearly reflects east coast origins. Developed in the mid 19th century such boats were fast, but with an upright stem and equally vertical stern were slow to answer the helm, and so not very manoeuvrable. A more refined hull shape was developed about 1880 for a design known as the Zulu that had a slightly raked bow and a steeply raked stern, not unlike a very large Loch Fyne skiff.

The herring industry reached its peak before the First World War and began an inexorable decline, accelerated by the war. Aware that islanders' boats were at a disadvantage compared to those based elsewhere, Cheshire soap magnate Lord Leverhulme tried to diversify the industry at Stornoway by introducing new ideas to the fishermen, but he was not made welcome. Undaunted he moved on, acquired the Harris Estate in 1919 and set up a large new fishing and canning enterprise at a location known as An t-Ob. He named his new port Leverburgh. He had rocks blasted away at sea to ease passage into the new pier where he built processing and canning sheds, a power station and houses. For a time it worked, but when Lord Leverhulme died in 1925 the enterprise had lost its driving force and closed. Abandoned, the buildings fell into dereliction, but one of Lord Leverhulme's fish-related businesses lasted longer. He opened a chain of shops known as Mac Fisheries, which became a familiar presence on high streets throughout Britain from 1918 until its demise in 1979.

The appearance of herring shoals off the Hebrides in May and June represented an early start to the season and small curing stations were set up at a number of locations around the islands, although the main effort was concentrated at Stornoway and the main harbour on the island of Barra, Castlebay. The name refers to Kisimul Castle, the forbidding looking stronghold of the chiefs of Clan MacNeil that sits out in the bay on a small rocky island and fills the background of this picture. Although small and somewhat isolated at the southern tip of the Outer Hebrides, Castlebay became sufficiently important to be recognised as a port of registry with the identifying letters CY. Every year the herring industry and the people who followed it around transformed the port and village. Some of these people were of course fishermen and because many of them were from the east coast, possibly including those in the picture, they swelled the numbers attending the Presbyterian Church on the mainly Catholic island. Boat crews often worked for curers under contract in the early boom years although later most preferred to operate independently and sell their catches to the highest bidder.

The curers were the herring boom's entrepreneurs who created the market and built the infrastructure to fill huge numbers of barrels with cured fish. They set up hutted accommodation for onshore workers, built the gutting troughs, supplied wood and employed coopers to make the barrels. On average a barrel held about 800 fish, and the mountains of barrels that appear in some of these pictures give an idea of the vast quantities of herring that were being caught and processed. The curers sold the fish and obtained the 'brand', which was stamped on the barrel as a mark of quality before being despatched to the customers. They also employed the female gutters and packers, the 'fisher lassies' who became an almost legendary part of the herring industry. Many of these women, perhaps most, were Scots and of those a large number were Gaelic-speaking islanders, including some from Barra. Theirs was an itinerant life because when the herring moved on after a couple of months or so, the curers also moved, packing up their huge travelling enterprise and relocating to any one of a number of ports round the British coast where the shoals were likely to appear.